Searching For The Light

Louise Lazenby

Presentation by *BookLeaf Publishing*

Web: www.bookleafpub.com

E-mail: info@bookleafpub.com

ISBN: 9789357440554

First edition 2023

Shine Bright, Silver Moon.

Shine bright, silver moon,
Glitter diamond stars,
For my love will be home soon,
And I'll be safe in his arms.

Glow warmly golden sun,
Light the bright blue sky,
Now I am with my chosen one,
With no more tears to cry.

Stand tall leafy trees,
Shelter the birds that sing,
Gentle whispers like a breeze,
A finger with a ring.

Blow strong autumn wind,
Drive the icy rain,
I trusted him, but he has sinned,
And caused me so much pain.

Fall heavy drifting snow,
And cover all the land,
For I have lost the life I know,
And the future we had planned.

A Double-sided Coin

A fine line between,
Love and hate, respect and scorn.
Two sides of one coin.

Nothing Left To Say

The love has blown away,
Driven by gales of icy words.
There's nothing left to say.

Resentments deep, hearts in decay,
Bitterness like poison,
The love has blown away.

Agony to leave, but torture to stay,
Torn by indecision.
There's nothing left to say.

Side by side like statues we lay,
Both hurting, never touching,
The love has blown away.

Playing out the same old script, in the same old
vicious way,
Until the words lose all their power and
There's nothing left to say.

Going into battle day after day,
Pride and Rage defeating Romance,
The love has blown away.
There's nothing left to say.

Poison

Cold and cruel he is.
She weeps bitter tears, bereft.
Home filled with poison.

Delusions

5

Your actions speak the truth, I know,
Words are meaningless in the face of them.
I cling to dreams of who I thought you were,
What I hoped we would become.
Delusions breaking piece by piece,
Small rips fraying larger day by day.
Cracks in my heart.
Sacrificing my future to validate the loss of my
youth.

Ignorance

Ignorance is bliss
I don't agree with this.
What you dont know cant hurt you
Just isnt true.
The hurt is still real,
Pain you still feel,
But you are left confused,
Living with consequences you didn't choose.
Feeling like a fool.
Not knowing the enemy to fight,
Scrabbling in the darkness,
Always searching for the light.

The Narcissist

Jagged words slice deep,
Hatred spat through gritted teeth.
Yet you say you bleed.

Ghosts

Some ghosts live in attics,
Swooping amongst the rafters,
But some ghosts torture the mind.

Some ghosts dwell in cellers,
Wailing into damp stones,
But some ghosts linger in memories.

Some ghosts float through forests,
Drifting between misty trees,
But some ghosts haunt the heart.

Some ghosts rage within buildings,
While some ghosts wander abroad,
But some ghosts besiege the soul.

Inertia

Inability to move forward,
No freedom to grow,
Everything seems so difficult,
Reluctance to make changes,
Too much fear to move on,
Impossible to see a different future,
A waste of a life.

The Illusion Of Freedom

Choice is limited.
Free will is an illusion.
The greatest deceit.

Magic

We once believed in giants,
And they strode across the land.
Climbing over mountains,
Grasping boulders in their hands.

We once believed in witches,
Who stirred their simmering brew.
Soaring over the treetops
And cackling as they flew.

We once believed in mermaids,
Gliding through the waves,
Luring ships towards the rocks,
Sinking sailors to watery graves.

We once believed in fairies,
Flitting through the glade,
Wings shimmering with magic,
Glowing in the shade.

We once believed in dragons,
Defeating knights so bold,
Breathing fire in towers and caves,
Guarding princesses and gold.

We once believed in fantasies,
In dreams and wishes and lore,
Now we believe what we are told to,
And the magic is no more.

All That Glitters

Beauty can mislead,
All that glitters is not gold.
Blinded by the light.

The Stalker

The great black dog they call me,
A beast you can't shake off your back,
But I am much more subtle than that,
Creeping, sinuous, pouncing - a cat.

Silently skulking and stalking,
I crouch in the shadows and wait,
Curled in broken heart and head,
Pacing the space with a silent tread.

Lightning-fast and vicious, suddenly I pounce,
Torturing emotions, like toying with a mouse.
Resilience shredded by sharpened claws,
Motivation battered by relentless paws.

The great black dog they call me,
A beast you can't shake off your back,
But I am much more subtle than that,
Creeping, sinuous, pouncing - a cat.

Peace

15

Velvet darkness soft,
Cocoon of isolation,
Peace in solitude.

The Price We Pay

How long should you wait,
For love to be given?
If respect has to be earned,
Kindness to be paid for,
Love to be negotiated,
Does this give it more value
Than that given freely
And without conditions?
In this world, we value things
By the price that is paid for them,
But should we pay with our hearts?
If it has cost our dignity,
Our peace of mind and our confidence,
Is it worth then more,
Than something simpler, something honest?
Should we cling to it all the harder,
Because it has cost us so dear?

A Perfect Storm

A perfect storm,
Is there such a thing?
Storms wreak destruction,
A violent dance of wind and rain,
Powerful pushing and pulling, merciless lashing,
Everything laid to waste.
A tempest of rage and recriminations,
Shouts of anger, tears of frustration and
heartbreak.
Everything built and everything grown brought
to ground.
Can it be remade, better stronger, more lovely,
Or will it stay a wasteland of broken dreams and
sharp edges?
Defying each attempt at a new beginning.

Know Your Value

A penny for your thoughts,
A ring for your heart,
How much does it cost to buy you,
To put a price on every part?
A thing is only worth what someone is willing to
pay.
Prices can change, day by day.
You are not a thing.
Know your value.

Inferno

Golden light flickers,
Building to an inferno.
Burning down the house.

Remember You Are Amazing

Spread your wings my angel,
Fly up, oh so high,
My heart is always with you,
Soaring through the sky.

Dream your dreams my darling,
Make them all come true,
Don't hide from your ambitions,
Be yourself in all you do.

Work so hard my precious,
Give it everything you've got,
But only give your energy
To things you love a lot.

Live your life my lovely,
Don't let anything hold you down,
Remember you're amazing,
Keep straightening your crown.

The Seasons

A promise of warmer days to come,
Carried on a cool breeze in the sunshine,
Blossoms drifting from trees like confetti,
Daffodils lifting their sunny faces to the light,
Paving the way for a riot of colour.

Luxurious days stretched to their limit.
Long, lazy evenings,
Walking barefoot on green grass,
Or salt-warm in the sunshine on soft sand.
Ice cubes clink as beads of water trickle down
the sides of your glass.

Orange leaves glow against a slate-blue horizon,
Fat raindrops fall from heavy skies,
A delight to cosy up at home,
While darker nights are still a novelty.
An indulgence to relax by the fire.

Crisp blue skies, air fresh and clean,
Each breath like toothpaste.
Making the most of precious daylight hours,
Long walks over frozen ground,
Not a second to be wasted.

Be Careful Who You Listen To

The pen is mightier than the sword,
Words have power to pierce
Hearts and minds like arrows.
Be careful who you listen to.

The tounge is crueler than the fist,
Words can linger for a lifetime,
Causing pain long after bruises heal.
Be careful who you listen to.

Ideas can be carried like weights.
Thoughts can be absorbed like poison.
Be careful who you listen to.